WHERE'S MY JOEY?

BY WENDY MONICA WINTER
ILLUSTRATED BY ROXANA CHITANU (ANTOCHI)

Illustrations and Graphic Design by Roxana Chitanu (Antochi)

Published by Wendy Monica Winter
ISBN 978-1-7773789-0-5
Squamish, British Columbia, Canada
V202203

ISBN/ISMN Published Heritage Branch
Library and Archives Canada /
Government of Canada

ISBN/ISMN, Direction générale du patrimoine publié
Bibliothèque et Archives Canada /
Gouvernement du Canada

For my sister in-law, Aurora Winter,
founder, www.samepagepublishing.com.
Her inspiration and guidance helped me and many other authors manifest their dream of writing their book.

Wendy Monica Winter

For Cornel, who always encourages and supports me on this creative journey.

Roxana Chitanu (Antochi)

ARCTIC OCEAN
GREENLAND
ATLANTIC OCEAN
U.S.A.
PACIFIC OCEAN
CANADA
U.S.A.
TIMOR SEA
DARWIN
the BUNGLE BUNGLES
GREAT SANDY DESERT
Lake Mackay
Lake Disappointment
Lake MacLeod
WESTERN AUSTRALIA
KATA TJUTA
Lake Carnegie
GREAT VICTORIA DESERT
PINNACLES
PERTH
INDIAN OCEAN
GREAT AUSTRALIAN BIGH
Australia

GULF OF CARPENTERIA
GREAT BARRIER REEF
PACIFIC OCEAN
ORTHERN
ERRITORY
QUEENSLAND
GREAT DIVIDING RANGE
SOUTH
USTRALIA
BRISBANE
Lake Eyre
NEW SOUTH WALES
BLUE MOUNTAINS
ADELAIDE
SYDNEY
the THREE SISTERS
CANBERRA
Mt. KOSCIUSZKO
MELBOURNE
TASMANIA
HOBART

Joeeeey!

Dinner time!

Where are you?

Where

could my little
one be?

Maybe...

my Joey
is behind that
tree.

Oh! It's you,
Ruby Rabbit!

Have you seen
my little Joey?

No. But I did see
some kids
playing earlier in
the flower fields.

No. Perhaps he is
in the ocean. We could hear
some laughter and splashes
from the Great Barrier Reef.

Hello, Emil Emu and
Ella Echidna. Have you,
by chance, seen my child?

I do hope
his dinner does not
get too cold.

Good to see you,
my friends. Whale, Turtle
and Ray, have you seen
my young one?

He was playing with
the Kookaburra Family,
earlier this morning.

Kookaburra Family, is Joey here?

No, I'm sorry to say that he left a long time ago. Joey said that he was going to phone some of his Canadian friends.

Have you heard from
my precious one?

We talked to him
earlier today. He said he would
visit Quinton Quokka.

Quinton Quokka,
do you know where Joey is?

No. Mamma Koala,
do you know where he is?

No, let me ask
my little one in my pouch.

Who is snoring
in my pouch?

Joey! I've been looking

everywhere

for you!

It's amazing that
I was looking
all over the
world

for something
that was always
inside
of me.

I love you.

WHERE'S MY JOEY ?

ARCTIC OCEAN
GREENLAND
ATLANTIC OCEAN
U.S.A.
PACIFIC OCEAN
CANADA
U.S.A.
TIMOR SEA
DARWIN
the BUNGLE BUNGLES
GREAT SANDY DESERT
Lake Mackay
Lake Disappointment
Lake MacLeod
WESTERN AUSTRALIA
KATA TJUTA
Lake Carnegie
GREAT VICTORIA DESERT
INDIAN OCEAN
PERTH
PINNACLES
GREAT AUSTRALIAN BIGH
Australia

CAN YOU SPOT ALL THE DIFFERENCES BETWEEN THE TWO MAPS?
VISIT WWW.WENDYMONICAWINTER.COM TO CHECK YOUR ANSWER.

Use Your Finger to Follow the Path

That Mother Kangaroo Takes to Find Her Joey

Did you notice that sometimes Mother Kangaroo had to go further away from Joey on her way to find him?

Wendy Monica Winter, M.Ed., is an award-winning author who lives with her husband, Calvin, in Squamish, British Columbia, Canada. Wendy enjoys bouncing around like Mamma Kangaroo. You can spot her big grin as she plays with kids at the park. She also likes to visit the local mountains to bounce on her mountain bike and even her skis!

She loves exploring new cultures and countries on our beautiful planet. In fact, travel inspired her to write her first book. While teaching in Perth, Australia, Wendy came up with this story, *WHERE'S MY JOEY?*.

This book is the first in her *WHERE'S MY* series so look for more playful and uplifting children's books from her.

For more information, please visit:
WWW.WENDYMONICAWINTER.COM

Roxana Chitanu (Antochi) is a self-taught Romanian illustrator living in Italy. As a child, she was often found in her grandparents' library, reading and looking at beautiful books. Now, through her art, she hopes to recreate those captivating havens for children.

Roxana loves animals, a good cup of coffee, and hiking with her husband.

Find out more about Roxana at:
WWW.ROXANAANTOCHI.COM / WWW.ROXANACHITANU.COM

Joey's Playful Pals

Kangaroo

Kangaroos are the largest of the marsupials (mammals that have pouches). Their only natural habitat is Australia.

Baby kangaroos, more affectionately called joeys, are born incompletely developed. When they are born, they are the size of a grape, have no ears or back legs, and are blind.

They will stay in their mother's pouch for the first six months as they continue to develop.

There can be two joeys in the pouch at once – one tiny and one fully developed.

Echidna

The echidna evolved over 20 million years ago and is one of the few mammals that lays eggs! This type of mammal is called a "monotreme." Echidnas have spikey quills on their body, so they look a bit like a porcupine. They are distant relatives of the platypus. They use their long snouts to find and gobble up worms, ants, and termites, but they don't have any teeth!

A baby echidna is called a "puggle." It hatches from an egg in its mother's pouch, and once it grows up, it spends its time digging, swimming, and climbing trees.

Emu

Due to its tiny wings, this bird cannot fly, but thanks to its long legs, the emu can sprint 50 kilometers per hour. Its long legs and tall neck make the emu the second tallest bird in the world. Can you guess which bird is the tallest in the world?

Usually, the male emu sits on the eggs. He does not eat or drink for about eight weeks while keeping the eggs warm.

The emu egg is so large that one egg can make an omelette to feed at least four people! Use the picture in the book to figure out the unusual color of emu eggs.

Quokka

The babies of these marsupials are also called joeys! Quokkas sleep during the day, which means they are nocturnal. They are also herbivores, which means they eat only plants. They mostly munch on grass and leaves and can even climb short trees for a snack. Like cows, they chew their cud.

These animals are not fearful of people and look like they are smiling, so they are known as very friendly animals. These inquisitive animals have a very limited distribution in the world; they can be mainly found on two islands off the western coast of Australia.

Kookaburra

You might think this bird is the silliest of Joey's friends because it is always laughing, but that's just its bird song! Kookaburras live in Australia and use their laughing sound to tell other kookaburras where their family's territory is. The family is made up of a mated pair and their grown-up babies who help them sit on eggs, find food, and protect the territory (until they are about 4 years old).

Kookaburras eat insects, worms, mice and even snakes. Sometimes kookaburras catch snakes and then kill them by clunking the snake's head on something hard!

Koala

The koalas are the laziest of Joey's pals because they are often sleeping! Koalas sleep up to 20 hours daily, staying safe in a tree, to digest their food. They eat eucalyptus leaves. Their hands and feet curl so they can hang on tightly to trees!

Did you know koala mothers also have a pouch, but their pouches face downward? Newborn koalas are as small as a jellybean and can't see or hear. They climb from the birth canal into their mother's pouch to continue growing, and then climb onto their mother's back.

LEARN MORE ABOUT THE JOEY'S PLAYFUL PALS, INCLUDING PRONUNCIATIONS AND FUN ANIMAL FACTS, AT WENDYMONICAWINTER.COM/PALS.

SOME PAGES FROM THE FIRST DRAFT OF THIS STORY

FOR MORE FUN,

CHECK OUT THE NEXT BOOK IN THE *WHERE'S MY?* SERIES

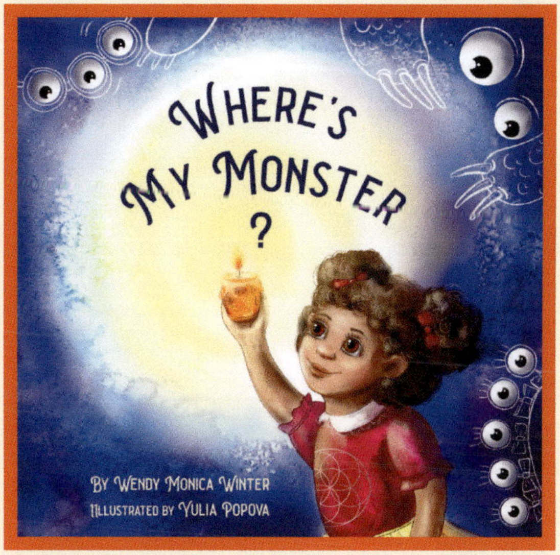

AND THE *WHERE'S MY JOEY? COLORING BOOK*

Printed in Great Britain
by Amazon

38115629R00023